The Brothers Grimm

Cinderella

and other fairy tales

Miles Kelly

First published in 2015 by Miles Kelly Publishing Ltd
Harding's Barn, Bardfield End Green, Thaxted, Essex, CM6 3PX, UK

2 4 6 8 10 9 7 5 3

Publishing Director Belinda Gallagher
Creative Director Jo Cowan
Editorial Director Rosie Neave
Designer Rob Hale
Production Elizabeth Collins, Caroline Kelly
Reprographics Stephan Davis, Jennifer Cozens, Thom Allaway
Assets Lorraine King

ISBN 978-1-78209-748-8

Printed in China

British Library Cataloguing-in-Publication Data
A catalogue record for this book is available from the British Library

ACKNOWLEDGEMENTS
The publishers would like to thank the following artists who have contributed to this book:

Front cover and all border illustrations: Louise Ellis (The Bright Agency)

Inside illustrations:
Cinderella Mónica Carretero (Plum Pudding Illustration Agency)
The Spirit in the Bottle Martina Peluso (Advocate-art)
The Glass Coffin Ayesha Lopez (Advocate-art)
The Magic Porridge Pot Polona Kosec (Advocate-art)

Made with paper from a sustainable forest

www.mileskelly.net
info@mileskelly.net

Contents

Cinderella

There was once a rich man whose wife died, leaving him with a daughter. He married again – a woman who had two daughters a little older than his own. However, his new wife was bad-tempered and spiteful – and her girls were just as nasty. How cruel they were to the man's daughter! They took her pretty clothes away and made her wear an old grey smock and wooden shoes. She was made to work hard from daybreak till nightfall in the kitchen, carrying water, lighting fires, cooking and washing. They made her sleep by the fireside in the ashes and, because she was always dirty with cinders, they called her Cinderella.

Poor Cinderella often felt miserable. Then, she would slip away to her mother's grave, where a beautiful hazel tree grew. She would sit by the grave, under the tree, for a while, and it always made her feel better.

One day, a trumpeter travelled through

the land announcing news from the king. There was going to be a festival lasting three days. All the young ladies in the country were invited, so that the prince could choose a bride.

The two stepsisters were delighted and immediately started to order Cinderella about. “Clean our shoes, help us into our dresses, fasten our necklaces and bracelets, and do our hair,” they instructed. Cinderella obeyed with tears in her eyes. She would have loved to go to the festival too, but

her stepmother had told her she was not allowed. In any case, she had nothing to wear.

The minute the horrid woman and her two ugly daughters had flounced out of the house, Cinderella went to her mother's grave beneath the hazel tree and sobbed.

Just then a little white bird swooped down out of the sky and landed on the tree. It threw down a beautiful embroidered dress and slippers! Cinderella's heart leapt with delight. She put on the dress and hurried off to the festival.

Everyone was at a ball there, dancing. Cinderella was so pretty in the embroidered dress that no one could take their eyes off her. She looked so different from when she was at home that her stepmother and stepsisters didn't recognize her – they thought she must be a foreign princess! As soon as the prince laid eyes on Cinderella he took her by the hand and danced with her. He didn't dance with anyone else all night! And if any other nobleman came to ask her to dance, he said, "No, she is *my* partner."

Cinderella danced till it was late, but she knew she had to be home before her stepmother and stepsisters. If they returned and found her gone, she would be in terrible trouble! When one of the ball guests was talking to the prince, Cinderella managed to slip away. She ran all the way to the hazel tree, and took off her beautiful clothes and shoes and laid them on her mother's grave. The little white bird picked them up and fluttered off with them while she put on her horrible smock and wooden shoes once more. Then she hurried home and took her place among the ashes.

When her stepmother and stepsisters returned, they could talk about nothing but the lovely foreign princess who had danced with the prince all night. "How I wish I could have seen her!" sighed Cinderella, keeping her secret safe in her heart.

The next day, Cinderella once again helped her stepmother and stepsisters into their party clothes. After they had left for the festival she went once again to her mother's grave. The little white bird swooped down with an even more lovely dress and slippers, made of silver cloth!

When Cinderella appeared at the ball in this dress, everyone was astonished by her beauty. The prince had not danced with anyone else, but had waited until she came. He instantly took her by the hand and danced with no one but her. And when other noblemen came to ask her to dance, he said, "No, she is *my* partner."

Once again, Cinderella danced till late in the night and then managed to slip away. The prince looked everywhere for her, but he could not find her! By the time her stepmother and stepsisters returned home, she was once more sitting in her work clothes in the ashes.

Then came the last day of the festival. Cinderella's stepmother and stepsisters went most excitedly, for tonight was the night that the prince would choose his bride.

Cinderella went to her mother's grave one more time and the little white bird swooped down with a golden dress and sparkling slippers even more splendid than before.

When Cinderella appeared at the ball in this dress, no one could speak for astonishment. The prince danced with her only, and if any one invited her to dance, he said, "No, she is *my* partner."

When it became late, Cinderella slipped

away. But the prince had laid a plan. He had ordered the staircase to be smeared with tar. Cinderella was so nimble that she did not stick fast – as the prince had hoped – but one of her shoes did, and she was forced to leave it behind.

The prince smiled as he picked up the shoe, even though Cinderella was running off into the night.

The next morning, the prince set out to find the girl whom the slipper fitted. He went from house to house, but no girl could squeeze her foot into the dainty shoe.

At last the prince came to Cinderella's house. How disappointed he was when he saw the two ugly stepsisters. It was clear that they wouldn't be able to fit their big, flat, clumsy feet into the shoe.

"Don't you have any other daughters?" he asked the rich man, in despair.

"Well... yes – one other," said Cinderella's father, uncertainly. "But she stays in the kitchen – she wasn't at the festival."

The prince didn't care – he demanded to see Cinderella at once.

Nervously, Cinderella went and bowed down before the prince, who gave her the shoe. She seated herself on a stool, drew her foot out of the heavy wooden shoe, and put it into the slipper – which fitted like a glove. And when she rose up and the prince looked at her face he recognized the beautiful maiden who had danced with him! "This is my bride!" he cried. He took Cinderella up on his horse and rode away with her – and they lived happily ever after.

The Spirit in the Bottle

Once there lived a poor woodcutter. He worked hard from morning until night to save money to send his son to school. The boy worked hard too and became very clever – but the money ran out before he could finish his studies. He had to return home to the woodcutter's hut in the forest.

"I am sorry, son," his father said, "I have no more money to give you – I hardly have enough to buy us food."

"Don't worry, Father," his son said brightly, "I can work hard. I don't mind chopping wood with you."

"But son, you're not used to such hard work," his father said sadly. "And besides, I have only one axe."

"Then see if your neighbour will lend you one, until I can make enough money to buy my own," the lad insisted.

So the woodcutter did and, next morning, the father and son went into the forest together. The lad got on with chopping wood quite merrily. When the sun was high in the sky, his father said, “Now we will rest and have our lunch.”

But his son said, “You rest, Father, I’m going to search for nuts and berries for our dinner,” and off he went through the trees.

During his search the lad came to an enormous oak tree. Then it seemed as if he heard a voice. It was very faint, but someone was crying: “Let me out! Let me out!” The lad looked around, but he couldn’t see anything. There it was again: “Let me out! Let me out!” It seemed like the voice was coming out of the ground! The boy searched around the tree roots – and there, half buried among the leaves and moss, he found an old glass bottle.

The lad brushed off the soil and held the bottle up to the light. There was a creature springing and spinning inside! "Let me out! Let me out!" it cried again, louder now and more desperate. So the boy hurried to draw the cork out of the bottle.

The creature slid through the neck of the bottle and began to swell... It grew and grew and grew...

until it became a mighty spirit. It towered over the lad and bellowed: "I was put into that bottle as a punishment. At first, I thought I would reward anyone who released me. But hundreds of years passed and as I waited I grew angrier and angrier – I swore I would kill the next person I met. And that is you – so now you must die!"

The boy was very afraid, but he was clever and he thought fast. "Actually," he said, "I can't see how you can have possibly been shut up in that bottle. You'd never fit inside! It must have been some sort of trick."

"What are you talking about?" roared the spirit. "Of course I was in there!"

"Prove it then," said the lad.

The spirit snorted with annoyance, and at once drew itself up... and shrank and shrank and shrank... until it became so tiny that it could slide back through the neck of the bottle and was once more jumping around inside again.

Quick as thought, the lad grabbed the cork, shoved it into the bottle, and the spirit was trapped once more. He shoved it back among the roots of the tree and went to walk away when the spirit cried out: “Set me free again and I promise you will never want for anything, for

the rest of your whole life!"

So the boy took the cork out again and the spirit rose up out of the bottle, growing in size until it towered over him once more.

Luckily, the spirit kept its word. "Here is your reward," it boomed, and it gave the lad a little bag with a sticking plaster in it. "This is a magic plaster," the spirit explained. "Put one end over any wound and it will heal. Put the other end over steel or iron and it will instantly change into silver." Then in a great puff of smoke the spirit vanished and the boy hurried back to his father.

“Where have you been?” the woodcutter asked. “We should have started work again ages ago.”

“Don’t worry, Father,” soothed the boy, “I will soon make it up to you.” He bent over his axe, so his father could not see what he was doing, and rubbed the iron blade with the magic plaster. It turned into gleaming silver! “Look at my axe, Father,” the boy said, holding it up. To his surprise, his father looked horrified instead of delighted.

“Oh my goodness, whatever’s happened!” the woodcutter gasped. “That’s no good for chopping trees any more – silver is softer than iron, it will just bend. I can’t give the axe back to my neighbour like that! You’ll have to go and sell it – you won't get much for a damaged axe though! I'll have to earn however much else we need to buy my neighbour a new one."

"Oh Father!" the son sighed, with a smile. He strode off into town and went straight to a jeweller. The jeweller gave him five thousand pounds for it!

The woodcutter's son went home delighted and asked his father how much his neighbour wanted for the axe. "Ten pounds," the woodcutter said, shaking his head sadly.

"Well, here's ten pounds," said the lad, counting out his money, "and here's many hundreds more!"

"Good heavens!" cried his father. "Where

on earth have you got all that money?"

Then the lad told him everything. The old woodcutter was thrilled – not only because he never had to worry about money again, but because his son could go back to school and finish his studies.

So he did – and because he could heal all wounds with his magic plaster, he became the most famous doctor in the whole world.

The Glass Coffin

There was once a young man who was learning to become a tailor, but he had always longed to have adventures, so one day he decided to go off travelling and see something of the world. But soon after he set off he became lost in a great forest. To make matters worse, he suddenly heard the sound of wild beasts roaring.

All at once a great black bull and a beautiful stag thundered through the trees towards him, their horns locked in a fight. The ground shook with their trampling and the air rang with their cries. For a long time the struggle seemed even, but at last, the stag thrust his antlers into the bull, which fell to the ground, dead.

To the tailor's astonishment, the stag then bounded up to him, swept him up on his great antlers, and carried him away. Over mountain and valley, wood and meadow they raced.

Just when the tailor thought he could hold on no longer, the stag came to a stop in front of a huge wall of rock, and gently let him down. Then the stag drove its antlers against a little door set into the rock and the door sprang open. Flames and smoke billowed out, then a deep voice boomed: "Enter!" The tailor drew up his courage and plunged through.

He found himself in a huge hall with a floor made of polished square stones. The voice boomed again: "Stand on the broad stone which lies in the middle of the hall."

Again the young man obeyed. He stood on the stone and it slowly gave way beneath his feet, carrying him down into the earth.

When the stone eventually stopped moving and the tailor looked around, he found himself in another hall, similar to the first. However, this hall had many hollows cut into the walls. In each one stood a glass vase, filled with blue gas. In the middle of the hall stood two big glass chests and the tailor strode over to look at them.

Inside the first was a model of a tiny castle, surrounded by a miniature village – tiny houses and farms, all perfectly detailed. Then he looked in the second glass chest. Inside lay the most beautiful young woman the tailor had ever seen!

She seemed to be fast asleep. But as the tailor stood gazing at her, she suddenly opened her eyes and looked straight at him!

"Oh thank goodness!" the lovely lady cried. "Someone's here at last! Please be quick – help me out of this prison. All you have to do is push back the bolt of this glass coffin and I will be free."

The young tailor hurried to release her.

"Oh thank you!" the beautiful young woman cried, sitting up and stepping out of the glass chest. To the tailor's delight she flung her arms around him and kissed him.

"Heaven must have guided you here to

help me. Please stay with me forever! I am the daughter of a rich nobleman," she explained. "My parents died when I was young and my elder brother and I stayed living in our castle, looking after each other. We were very happy, with the kind villagers around us. Then one evening a stranger came to the castle and asked for my hand in marriage. I turned him down, which made him very angry. He muttered black magic and I fell to the ground in a faint.

"When I came to, I found myself in this cave in the glass coffin. The stranger – and by now I had realized he was a wicked magician – appeared again and said he had changed my brother into a stag. He had shrunk my castle and village into a tiny model and set it in the other glass chest. And he had turned all my people into smoke and trapped them in glass bottles.

"He told me that he would give me one more chance. If I would now marry him, he would turn everything back the way it was – all he had to do to break the spell was to get everything out of the glass... But I couldn't say yes to such an evil monster! So he vanished, leaving me here in my prison. I fell into a deep, enchanted sleep. But at last, you have arrived and set me free!

"Now please help me lift the glass chest with my castle in it on to that broad stone."

The young tailor did so at once. Straight away the stone began to rise up and up... until they were in the higher hall, and could carry the chest out into the open air. Here, the young woman opened the lid. The two watched in amazement as the castle, houses, and farms grew before their eyes, returning to their normal sizes and places.

After this, the young woman and the tailor returned to the lower cave and fetched all the glass bottles.

Nervously, the lady opened them one by one. The blue smoke rushed out and instantly changed into living men, women and children. As they hugged each other, laughing delightedly, a handsome young man came striding out of the forest.

The beautiful noblewoman gasped and tears of joy sprang to her eyes. It was her brother! They ran to each other at once and the brother explained that the evil magician was gone forever. He had transformed himself into a bull whom, as the stag, the brother fought and killed. He had then brought the young tailor here, in the hope that he would release his sister from the glass coffin. As the tailor had done so, the brother had been set free from his enchantment too.

Then everyone's joy was complete. On that very day, the beautiful noblewoman married the tailor, and they lived with her brother in the castle happily ever after.

The Magic Porridge Pot

There was once a little girl who lived in a cottage on the edge of a forest with her mother. They were very poor – so poor that the day came when they no longer had anything to eat. The little girl went into the forest, crying with hunger, to see if there were any berries or nuts she could gather. As she was searching, someone came hobbling towards her through the trees. It was an old woman, carrying a little cooking pot.

"Don't cry, dear," said the old woman, kindly. "Take this little pot and go back home. Whenever you say, 'Little pot, cook!' it will cook tasty porridge." The little girl couldn't believe her eyes – steaming hot porridge started to bubble up in the pot as the woman spoke. "Whenever you say, 'Little pot, stop!' " the old woman continued, "it will stop cooking." And the pot stopped cooking, full to the brim of thick, creamy porridge waiting to be eaten.

The little girl thanked the old woman wholeheartedly for her wonderful gift and hurried home with the magical pot to show her mother at once.

From then on, the little girl and her mother could have hot porridge whenever they wanted, and they never had empty tummies again.

One day, when the little girl had gone to a friend's house to play, her mother felt hungry and said, "Little pot, cook!" And the porridge instantly appeared and began to bubble and rise to the brim.

But for some reason, the mother could not remember the exact words to make the pot stop. "Stop, little pot!" she ordered. But the magic pot kept cooking. The mother tried every command she could think of: "Stop, small pot!... Small pot, stop! Enough, small pot! Small pot, enough! No more, little pot..."

But still the pot kept cooking and cooking and the porridge kept rising and rising. Soon it flowed over the edge of the pot and onto the floor, and it went on until the whole kitchen was flooded.

When the entire floor was covered the porridge began to spread out into the street. Then the sticky goo flowed into the house next door, and the next, and the next – and still it kept coming. Everyone was crying and wading through porridge, and no one knew how to stop it.

When the porridge was about to flood the last house in the village, the little girl came home. “Little pot, stop!” she commanded firmly – and the pot stopped cooking at once.

Then everyone had to eat the village clean!